Horncastle

on old picture p

GW00650175

Eric Cro

1. The sweet shop of a Miss Cussons (who is presumably standing in the doorway) at 20 The Bull Ring. Unfortunately, in a modernisation of the property at some time, it acquired neo Georgian windows and the attractive first floor windows and box guttering were removed. It now claims to be *"the home of the famous Lincolnshire plum loaf"*!

INTRODUCTION

HORNCASTLE is an attractive and historic market town in the Lincolnshire Wolds, midway between Lincoln and the coast. In Roman times it was known as Banovallum, which name you will see used in the town today, for example the Banovallum School. It derives its present name from the Saxon "Hyrne-Ceaster" which translates to "castle on the promontory". In recent years historians have, however, suggested that these names might be better associated with Caistor, another Lincolnshire Wolds town, but this cannot be pursued in a book based on 20th century postcards!

The church of St. Mary is situated in the town centre, off the Market Place, but in spite of its large tower, it can hardly be called a landmark as it is almost tucked away!

The town was once famed for the Great Horse Fair which was held in August and reputedly the largest horse fair in England. It was also noted for the number of public houses, according to a local gentleman, who claimed it had more pubs than any other town of similar size!

Just as it was famed for the horse fair and perhaps the number of pubs, it is now noted for the number of antique shops and claims to be the antiques centre of the East Midlands. There are certainly a lot of them, but very few selling postcards! The River Bain, River Waring and the Old River Bain all meet here and on more than one occasion this century the town has suffered serious flooding.

In the first decade of the 20th century, Horncastle's population was just over 4,000. Important trade took place in corn and wool, while malting and brewing were key industries. This book provides a flavour of life at that time as seen on picture postcards. A selection of post-1920 cards is also included.

Picture postcards were first published in Britain in 1894, but did not become really popular until in 1902 Post Office regulations were changed to allow the message to be written on the back of the card along with the address. From then until the outbreak of World War One in 1914, postcards had a 'Golden Age,' with upwards of two million being posted nationally each day. They were a cheap and efficient way of sending urgent messages or gossip before the telephone became widely-used, and the huge variety of images on the picture side of the cards - transport, events, personalities, street scenes - made them very collectable. Most families had their own albums for saving these attractive cards, whether received through the post or bought specially for the collection. Even after 1914, the postcard habit was well established, and cards continued to be sent in large numbers. Views were published of every subject from royalty to actresses, country houses to suburban back streets. Horncastle was fortunate in the quality of postcards published, for while most towns had a local photographer who published postcards, Horncastle had several. The cards produced by Mr Hick and Miss Blades were good but those by Carlton & Son were superb, as you will see in the following pages. Strangely, though, the town's railway station (at the end of a branch line which ran off the Great Northern Railway's route from Lincoln to Peterborough) was apparently not covered by any of these photographers. Where known, the names of postcard publishers are included within each caption.

Eric Croft
October 1999

Front cover: High Street at the junction with the Bull Ring, on a picture postcard published by Carlton about 1906. So good is the photography that every shop sign and advertisement is readable. On the left are Metcalfe's Commercial Hotel, then Carlton's druggist shop, Booth Redmore's hat & caps shop, and Achurch, iron-monger.

BRIDGE STREET. HORNCASTLE

2. Bridge Street (facing South) with Hare & Co.'s shop on the left. This postcard was published by Ruddocks of Lincoln in 1908 when Lightowler's hairdressers occupied the corner of Hare's building. A hoarding outside advertises tobacco and cigarettes.

COPYRIGHT NCE. 14.   EAST STREET, HORNCASTLE.   LILYWHITE LTD. TRIANGLE, HALIFAX

3. East Street from the junction with South Street and The Bull Ring. Mrs Pogson's corsets, wool and underclothing shop was demolished with other buildings after suffering damage in the 1960's flood. Card published by Lilywhite of Halifax in the 1920's.

4. West Street on a Lilywhite's postcard posted at Horncastle in 1932. The white building on the right is 'The Crown' public house. The building in the left foreground, then an 'authorised Ford dealer', has been replaced with a modern car showroom.

5. The "Bridge Foot" Stores of E. Brown on a c. 1905 postcard by local photographer V.M. Hick. The shop front has been rebuilt from the ground to the roof and the rest of the brickwork painted - what a shame.

6. North Street on a Carlton & Sons postcard c. 1910. The building on the right was the Court House at this time (now the job centre) and the one opposite is the hospital. The horse and cart carries the name T. Harrison & Son, who were merchants in corn, coal, seeds and artificial manure!

High Street, Horncastle

7. High Street from the Bull Ring, with the 'Red Lion' on the right. Thorpe & Robinson's shop is on the right. The postcard, published by Scottish firm G.W. Wilson, comes from a time when standing in the road was not a problem!

8. North Street on another card by Carltons but taken near the junction with The Bull Ring. One of my favourite postcards!

9. Bridge Street (facing North) with perhaps the county's most decorative warehouse building on the left (now Hare & Co's furniture showroom). It was built in 1864 and used for the storage of corn, wool etc. The white painted cottage on the right is no longer there and has been replaced with a dreadful 1960's style shop! This postcard was published by Valentine of Dundee and posted to Fulstow in December 1903. *"If you come on Saturday it will suit us nicely"*, wrote the sender, *"We will meet the train that arrives in Donington a little after three."*

10. High Street, this time on a W. H. Smith postcard published about 1910. The shops of Redmore and Maynard are prominent on the right.

MARKET PLACE. HORNCASTLE.

11. Market Place on a Ruddock postcard c. 1910. The white buildings on the right have been replaced but all the others have survived. The shop which then carried the *W. Bryant* sign now bears a plaque to inform us that Sir Joseph Banks, botanist with Captain Cook, lived here. Morton & Sons' shop is centre right of the picture.

1082 High Street, Horncastle.

12. High Street in 1916 with the Corn Exchange on the right, one of the few buildings in the street which has not survived. The site is now occupied by a modern supermarket. The Corn Exchange also served as the 'Victory Cinema.' At the end is the agricultural ironmongers' shop of James Ward. This appears on a number of postcards in this volume! The postcard is one of a long series, probably published by Jackson of Grimsby.

13. High Street looking towards the Market Place; judging by the activity, it was Market Day. The view is much the same today - even the Town Clock on its ornate bracket has survived.

14. High Street - a sister card to no. 12, almost certainly photographed on the same day. The Corn Exchange/Cinema is now on the left, with Rowbotham's boot & shoe store on its right. It was posted at Lincoln in June 1925.

15. Bull Ring from the East/South Street junction on a card published by E. Peakome of Boston showing part of the South Bridge on the left. Unfortunately the bridge has been replaced with a concrete and metal structure with a wire mesh "railing"!

BULL RING. HORNCASTLE.

16. The Bull Ring on a J.W. Ruddock card posted in 1908. The 'Red Lion' on the left has lost a bay window and the opening widened. The small white painted building in the centre was the 'Fleece Inn' but it closed in the 1960's and is now a shop.

ST. MARY'S SQUARE. HORNCASTLE.

17. St Mary's Square on another Ruddock card, which was posted to Worksop in 1908. This attractive street, which has featured on numerous picture postcards, has hardly changed, except that some of the thatch on the cottages on the left has been sheeted over.

18. Mr Stevenson's "Victoria Roller Flour Mills" on a V.M. Hick postcard, published c. 1905. The mill building has survived, although it is looking somewhat derelict. The River Bain has been diverted to the left of the mill, and it is now quite picturesque, with its landscaped banks and trees.

19. "On the Bain". With two rivers and a canal converging in such a small area the photographs were confused. This card could be titled *The River Waring* or *The Canal* but not *The River Bain*. Some years ago these banks were replaced with concrete walls and the scene now looks dreadful. The buildings have gone except for the 'Ship Inn' in the distance. This card was published by Harrison of Lincoln.

20. A soldier is featured rowing down The Canal on a card posted in 1917! The building on the right is now a youth centre but was originally Cagthorpe School.

21. The Canal, again from South Bridge, facing west, showing how tranquil this area used to be. The card, published by W.K. Morton, was posted in June 1920, and the message reads *"...it has been terrible here with the floods"*.

22. The South Bridge is called Boston Bridge on this c. 1905 postcard. The large building on the right was demolished after suffering damage in the floods of 1960. At this time the sign reads J.T. Eyre, but this name does not appear in any contemporary directory.

BULL RING, FROM NORTH ST., HORNCASTLE   Photo. Martineau

23. A more up to date view of the Bull Ring, published by Martineau and dating from the late 1950's. The 'Fleece Inn' on the right sold Flowers Ales.

24. Coronation Day celebrations 1911 in the Market Place on a postcard published by Miss A. Blades, Queen Street, Horncastle. Even the milkman had stopped to have a look!

25. The Coronation celebrations again, but this card was published by Carlton.

26. The Bull Ring on yet another Carlton
and the 'King's Head' on the left.

he 'Red Lion' is centre distance,

27. Another Coronation Day postcard, also published by Carlton. The soldiers in the foreground are aiming their rifles in the air, but judging by the puffs of smoke in the background some had already been fired.

28. Not to be left out, Mr Hick was also there with his camera. This card shows more clearly the Stanhope Memorial. It is a 30ft. high structure with granite columns erected in 1898 to the memory of Edward Stanhope. He was MP for the town for about 19 years. I can't imagine any of today's MPs being remembered in this way!

The Horncastle Flood of 1920

Lincolnshire people and postcard collectors all over the country will have heard of the Louth floods of 1920, when some 20 people were drowned, and a long series of picture postcards was published depicting scenes of the events. Few outside Horncastle, though, will remember or have heard of the flood that hit the town on the same day, May 29th 1920. Following a cloudburst, both Louth and Horncastle were severely flooded. The *Daily News* headlines on 1st June read *"Louth Flood Disaster - hundreds homeless, 20 dead."* The effect on Horncastle was far less traumatic for the residents, and there was no loss of life. The obvious publicity and attention was directed at Louth, and events at Horncastle went almost un-noticed. Some years ago, I bought a handful of postcards which appeared to have been produced by an amateur photographer. As a result, they were probably published in small quantities, and are thus extremely scarce.

29. The town's manually operated fire engine which, according to the note, is *"pumping out water at the 'Punch House'"*. Was it because they were at a pub that it took 14 men and a boy to work the engine?! 'The Punch House' has now been renamed 'The Victorian.'

30. The note reads *"Pike's House after the water had gone down on Sunday morning"*. The height of the flood water is marked *x x* on the windowsill of the building on the right. George Pike is listed in Kelly's Directory as House Furnisher, Glass & China Warehouseman, Decorator, Paperhanger, Builder, Undertaker, Cabinetmaker and Upholsterer! As the building is now an Antiques Centre, perhaps some of Mr Pike's wares are now on sale again!

31. The note tells us that this is *"Hensman's pit which took tons of water"*. It is referring to Charles Hensman and Son of The Becks who were brick and tile manufacturers.

32. This shows the flood water in Bridge Street with 'The Punch House' in the background. The note just reads *"Lunn & Dodson's Shop in the flood"*.

33. The note on this rather murky photograph reads *"West Street after the flood"*.

34. *"Kirkham's Shop with the pavement washed up"*, is the note on this card. The shop is situated almost at the corner of Bridge Street and West Street, opposite the Antiques Centre.

35. This shows the same building from the opposite direction, but this card was published by Harrison's of Lincoln, and is the only professionally produced postcard of the floods I have seen.

36. This is Prospect Street, and the height of the flood is marked on the arched doorways at shoulder height to these men. The warehouse building in the background has gone.

37. This is Geo. Marshall's shop at the corner of Bridge Street and West Street. It was perhaps demolished after the flood and it has not been rebuilt. The same shop can also be seen on illus. 28 and 33.

38. Here we have a more detailed note, which reads *"Browns Studio, Bridge Street. Since photo was taken the place has partly collapsed and is now being taken down".* I think that this building was on the riverside at the back of E. Brown's shop (illus. 5). The notice in the window reads: *C A Brown - Car for hire.*

39. The local Salvation Army band from the Edwardian era on a postcard published by Miss A. Blades of 18 Queen Street, Horncastle.

Mrs Horncastle : Archibald ! Certainly NOT !

40. There are a few of these political comic cards, all of a similar type. The card, published by Duttons of Skegness, was posted in Peterborough in February 1911 and the message reads *"The only card handy which the Radicals issued during the Horncastle election."* The cartoon refers to the December 1910 election, the second of that year, the result of which enabled prime minister Asquith to reduce the power of the House of Lords. Linfield was the Liberal winer of the Horncastle seat, and Tory candidate Weigall is sent packing back to Gainsborough. *"Archibald! Certainly not!"* is a reference to a contemporary music-hall song.

41. This card was published during the January 1910 general election. The brass plate reads *"Horncastle Division Conservative Association"*. The window displays various posters for "Willoughby" and the one on the pram reads *"Stick to my daddy's candidate"*. The illustrated posters in the window and on the wall also appeared as a series of picture postcards.

42. The Hunt meeting in the Bull Ring on another Carlton card, posted at Horncastle in March 1908. All the buildings are still here including the little canopy on the right! Ward's shop is in the centre distance. The message on the back reads: *"Thought this P.C. might interest you - see if you can find anyone you know!"*

43. PC 79L, who we know from the note on the back is P.C. Lusby - Mrs Redmore's father. The photographer was Mr Hick.

44. This proud looking fireman had his photograph taken by Miss Blades and it carries the message *"with Fireman Brown's compliments"*.

HORNCASTLE FAIR, SOUTH BRIDGE & WATERSIDE.

45. The famous horse fair on a Carlton's card posted in 1910. This and the following are printed, rather than photographic, so the publisher obviously thought he would sell a lot of them!

HORNCASTLE, FAIR. BULL RING & HIGH STREET.

46. The horse fair in the High Street. Just imagine several hundred horses thronging the town centre in the hot weather! Card published by Carlton & Sons.

47. Another horse fair scene, this time on a postcard published by Miss Blades. It shows scores of horses in the Bull Ring in July 1915 and the rear ends of two more in the foreground!

48. The Church Lads Brigade on an undated card by W.K. Morton, numbered 36. This company still produces the *"Horncastle News"*.

49. A postcard by Carlton, uncaptioned as usual. A note on the reverse reads *"Horncastle's first aeroplane landed down Green Lane"*. There were actually two Green Lanes but I have not been able to pinpoint this exact location.

50. This event, featured on another Carlton postcard, was obviously a novelty, but the crowd is by no means huge.

A consignment of Albion & Deering Binders arrive at Horncastle Station
for E. Achurch & Sons.

51. Horncastle Station, and at least sixteen binders arriving for Achurch & Sons. The name continues in the town today with a shop in the Market Place. This is the only postcard I have seen, or even heard of, featuring Horncastle Station. Who's got them all?

52. Miss Blades was out with her camera again and this time to photograph General Bramwell Booth. Is there anywhere he didn't visit?

53. The five sail mill on Spilsby Road in its heyday. Only the tower has survived but even this has lost two storeys! Card published by G.W. Wilson.

Five Sail Mill, at Horncastle

54. This is the six sail mill which stood on Louth Road and of which nothing remains. Photographic postcard by Hick.

55. The 1st Banovallum scout troop photographed by Miss Blades. The card was posted in the town in 1912, and sent to Nettleham.

56. A different group of scouts who commissioned Carltons to take their photograph!